YOUR KNOWLEDGE HAS VALUE

AF143985

- We will publish your bachelor's and master's thesis, essays and papers

- Your own eBook and book - sold worldwide in all relevant shops

- Earn money with each sale

Upload your text at www.GRIN.com and publish for free

Biased Algorithms in Law Enforcement Agencies. A Case Study of the LA Police Department

Julian Schoenemeyer

Bibliographic information published by the German National Library:

The German National Library lists this publication in the National Bibliography; detailed bibliographic data are available on the Internet at http://dnb.dnb.de.

ISBN: 9783346848796
This book is also available as an ebook.

© GRIN Publishing GmbH
Nymphenburger Straße 86
80636 München

Print and binding: Books on Demand GmbH, Norderstedt, Germany
Printed on acid-free paper from responsible sources.

The present work has been carefully prepared. Nevertheless, authors and publishers do not incur liability for the correctness of information, notes, links and advice as well as any printing errors.

GRIN web shop: https://www.grin.com/document/1334829

Biased Algorithms in Law Enforcement Agencies

A Case Study of the LA Police Department

Final Essay

submitted by

Julian Schoenemeyer

Faculty of Social Sciences

Security and Technology Seminar

Prague, 16.01.2023

Contents

1. Surrounded by Algorithms

In today's society, we are constantly surrounded by artificial intelligence, especially by algorithms that try to profile us to predict our future behaviour. These algorithms are deeply embedded in our daily lives, whether we are watching Netflix, using Amazon music or do online shopping, they try to present us with suggestions to get us more involved with the platform to spend more time there and therefore more money. But these algorithms are not only operated by business companies alone, they are also implemented with public policy providers and law enforcement agencies, like police forces. Can these algorithms be always fair and impartial? How are they used within the police force to profile criminality? These are the most important questions that I try to answer in this paper.

At first, the functioning of an algorithm has to be explained further. In one sentence, an algorithm is a set of commands that helps computers to interpret specific information that lead the system to a certain decision (*Algorithmic Bias*, 2023). The problem with algorithms being biased lies within the programming processes itself. First of all, it is based on existing available data within society that might be biased already. Take for example an algorithm that tries to match job offers with unemployed people. It draws first upon the data on what kind of CV the current people have who work in this specific job branch and tries to match these findings with possible applicants who match those criteria (*Algorithmic Bias*, 2023). Is the majority of the already employed people male and white, then the algorithm might view this specific type of human as the ideal one and would therefore reproduce and advance this specific socio-economic pattern (*Algorithmic Bias*, 2023). This example shows, what extreme effects algorithmic choices can have on society by reproducing biased patterns extensively. Moreover, these algorithms are not only restricted to the job market but extends also into the security sector, strongly influencing law enforcement agencies.

A very present example of applied algorithms in the security sector might be as a facial recognition software. We are constantly surrounded by it without recognizing that it is there. All the time we are passing by a camera in public, we might get scanned by a facial recognition software. It can also be a threat to our basic right, based on the programming database of the applied algorithm. It can scan according to the preferences set by the underlying database, i.e., skin colour, gender etc.

A really striking example for how far the use of algorithms in law enforcement environment goes, is the fact that judges are using AI to hand down sentences in court (*Algorithmic Bias*, 2023). This method is comparable with the `predictive policing´ technique that is elaborated further later in the text. With `predictive sentencing´ the algorithm takes existing criminal cases and considers the specific information about the offender to come to a decision in the end (*Algorithmic Bias*, 2023). Specific data points are: Socioeconomic status, neighbourhood, family background and a risk assessment questionnaire (*Algorithmic Bias*, 2023). By just looking at the data points the algorithm uses, one can clearly identify that there is a lot of space for bias with the algorithm developing specific discriminatory criteria based upon ethnic affiliation and therefore gives biased sentences.

Another example might be, that algorithms decide in the US what patrol routes the police officers are supposed to take to minimize the risk of crime. This specific method is called `predictive policing´ (*Algorithmic Bias*, 2023). The arrests of the past are determining the route of the police patrol. Apparently, on basis of these possible applications, security algorithms bear a lot of possibilities for discriminating against a certain group of people that the computer is targeting upon from its database. With the `predictive policing´ algorithm, the police is likely to police certain areas too heavily that are inhibited by specific ethnic minorities (*Algorithmic Bias*, 2023). Drawn from this concept, it is more likely that arrests happen there where the police is spend most of the time and these arrests are fed to the system. Then, the algorithm adjust the policing routes according to these new data and reinforces discrimination and inequality of these ethnic minorities (*Algorithmic Bias*, 2023). In support of this theory, the official data from the U.S. Department of Justice of 2018 shows that black people are overrepresented in the statistic being arrested for nonfatal violent crimes and for serious nonfatal crimes relative to the white U.S. population (Dr. Beck, 2021). That might indicate algorithmic fostered inequality already. This correlation can be found in the empirical data below that are drawn from the statistical brief.

TABLE 1

Race or ethnicity of the U.S. resident population and of persons arrested for nonfatal violent crimes, 2018

Race/ethnicity	U.S. resident population, July 1, 2018	Persons arrested, UCR 2018	
		Nonfatal violent crimes[a]	Nonfatal violent crimes excluding other assault
White[b]	60.4%	45.9%	38.7%
Black[b]	12.5	33.0	36.1
Hispanic	18.3	17.6	21.4
American Indian/ Alaska Native[b]	0.7	1.9	1.9
Asian[b]	5.7	1.3	1.5
Native Hawaiian/ Other Pacific Islander[b]	0.2	0.3	0.4
Two or more races[b]	2.2	--	--

Table 1:Levels of criminality within different ethnic groups

Source: U.S. Department of Justice, https://bjs.ojp.gov/library/publications/race-and-ethnicity-violent-crime-offenders-and-arrestees-2018

The above-mentioned examples of algorithmic use within the law enforcement branch shows how far AI is impacting our society already. But are they more supportive to the agencies or do they more harm to whole society at all? The problem that causes strong bias within algorithmic decisions lies within the database that features embedded inequalities already. The program itself can be good, but it can´t make justified decisions based on a biased dataset that was created on wrong data. On the other hand, algorithmic bias can also be detected when data is correct (*Algorithmic Bias*, 2023). This can happen when the code behind the algorithm weights specific discriminatory elements higher in its calculations than non-discriminatory ones. Therefore, it can still lead to a biased decision that discriminates against certain ethnic minorities. In addition, it is often very hard for the public to determine if an algorithm consists out of discriminatory elements because no everyone is a programmer and can understand these publicly operating algorithms (*Algorithmic Bias*, 2023). Furthermore, the source code of these algorithms is not publicly available. Most of all, human bias is often embedded within algorithms because algorithms are developed by humans in the end. This is the biggest danger of all that human bias can´t be mitigated perfectly.

To conclude, it is apparent that algorithms in law enforcement agencies can be insufficient and lead to a biased outcome. To be able to answer the research questions from the beginning and to test the correlations mentioned above, I will draw upon a specific case study in the next chapter. The following case study is dedicated to empirically examine how algorithms are implemented within law enforcement agencies in the US and if they might bear an internal discriminatory bias already that affects its decision.

2. Methodology

For my research design, I have chosen a qualitative single case approach. According to my questions, I can best test the implications of AI within law enforcement agencies best by using this method. My research design is an interrupted time series design, reaching from the time before the introduction of the algorithm until the current status. As a case study I picked the LA police department as it is the third biggest police department in the US. Therefore, it has a lot of impact on society as well as the resources to implement AI into their daily processes. As a further justification for my case study, it is worth mentioning that Los Angeles has a big population of roughly 3.8 Mio. inhabitants and a large portion of its citizens are part of an ethnic minority. According to the 2022 census, the whites are becoming an ethnic minority itself whit only representing 29% of the total population of the city (Pallini-Tipton, 2023). The Hispanics are now the dominant ethnic group in the city surpassing the whites by representing 48% of the total population of the city (Pallini-Tipton, 2023). The two other remaining significant ethnic minority groups are Asians accounting for 12% and Blacks accounting for 8% of LA citizens (Pallini-Tipton, 2023).

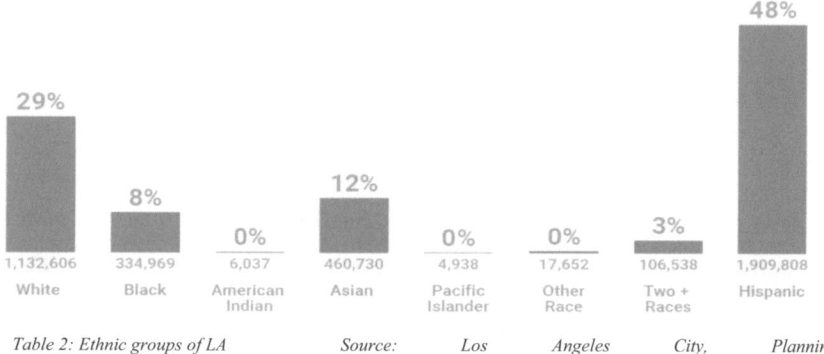

Table 2: Ethnic groups of LA   Source: Los   Angeles   City,   Planning,
https://planning.lacity.org/resources/demographics

Next, it is worth mentioning that the LA police department has already experience with using AI in its daily routine. To apply predictive policing methods in their department, the police has used special algorithmic programs, called Operation LASER and Palantir. I will quickly elaborate further on both programs. Operation LASER stands for Los Angeles Strategic Extraction and Restoration program. It was part of the LAPD as a smart policing initiative to reduce gun violence (Craig & Swatt, 2013). This algorithm is based upon two critical elements. At first, it checks if someone is a chronic offender and secondly, it consists out of a chronic location component (Craig & Swatt, 2013). The main goals of this predictive policing algorithm are diverse. It should help to extract offenders from critical neighbourhoods and restore peace there (Craig & Swatt, 2013). Furthermore, it should secure that gun offenders can be identified and reveal the identity of gang members (Craig & Swatt, 2013). Overall, it tries to secure a reduction in gun and gang-related crime (Craig & Swatt, 2013). Its theoretical background are the situational and environmental theories of crime (e.g., Felson, 2002). Technically, it is supposed to target repeated gun offenders and gang members in the target areas with laser-like precision to be able to extract them (Craig & Swatt, 2013). It is doing that by the use of a point system that gets suspects points on the LASER score according to their criminal record. If they are a gang member for example, they get 5 points on it (Craig & Swatt, 2013). They get the same amount if they were arrested before and if they are getting checked upon, they receive one additional point (Craig & Swatt, 2013). In addition, the individual gets 5 points when it is on probation and it gets 5 points when it has conducted past crimes (Craig & Swatt, 2013). Apparently, this algorithm features self-enforcing mechanisms as well that leaves space for biased policing.

Note from the editor: This image was removed due to copyright issues.

Figure 1: LASER predicted gun-related criminal hotspots in Newton Area in 2011; Source: Uchida and Swatt 2013

Source: https://journals.sagepub.com/doi/10.1177/1098611113497044

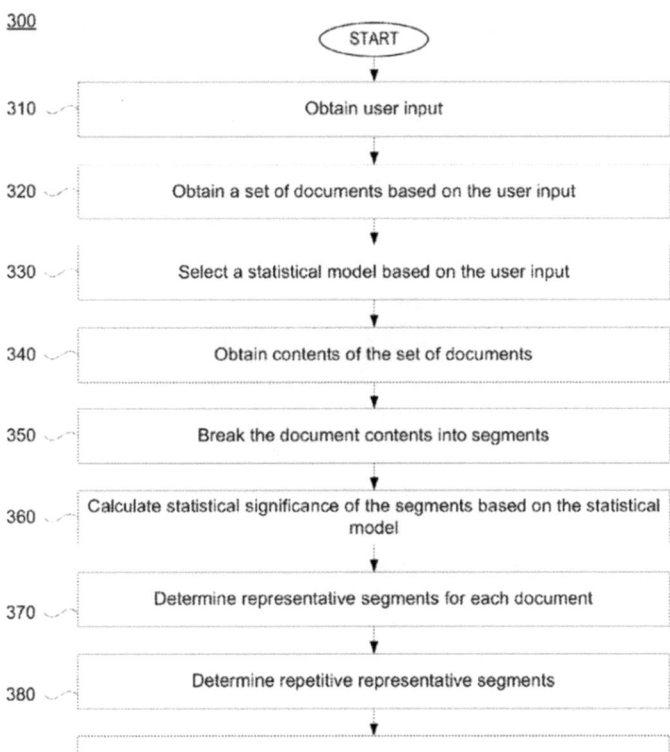

Figure 2: Process model of the Palantir algorithm; Source: PALANTIR TECHNOLOGIES, INC.,
https://www.patentsencyclopedia.com/app/20110072003

Palantir serves as a connector between several major databases that law enforcement agencies use in Los Angeles and across the whole state (Cushing, 2020). The data spreads out over a wide array of different sources. These sources include incident reports, arrests, citations, license plates, field interviews, recovered vehicles, warrants, booking photos, telecommunications and health service data (Cushing, 2020). After combining all these pieces of data, Palantir organizes the data algorithmically to find possible links between the people in the database (Cushing,

2020). It is not easy to explain the algorithm in detail and how it works exactly, but a look in the patent from Palantir can help further. So, at least parts of the algorithm are publicly available since it is used within public agencies. The most important element of the algorithm is, that it uses key phrase characterization of documents of a plurality of documents to develop a specific statistical model to calculate a statistical significance (Kesin & Wadhar, 2015). Part of this statistical calculation is to determine repetitive representative segments what can be viewed as a mathematical reconstruction of the person (Kesin & Wadhar, 2015). To exemplify this technically, a police officer is able to reconstruct all the data about a person by just searching for the smallest piece of evidence that can be found on the controlled individual to reconstruct the person virtually and to determine its future behaviour. It is hard to say without being a programmer if the algorithm makes decisions based on a biased statistical model, but what is for sure, that the model features repetitive elements. The system can probably discriminate based on how many times a person was already interviewed or on health service data.

The use of these methods stresses the relevance for a case study targeting the LA Police Department, because the consequences of a biased algorithm can be tremendous in a city that is inhabited by so many different ethnicities. This circumstance can also justify why the case is perfect to examine if algorithms can foster inequalities and discrimination within ethnic minority groups.

3. Case Study

Now that I have outlined both algorithmic driven predictive policing methods the LAPD uses, their impact needs to be tested within the LAPD. I will test both methods regarding their effectiveness in reducing crime levels and how they correspond to discriminatory factors.

At first, I am starting with a case study about the LASER program. Therefore, I draw on Craig´s and Swatt´s study from 2013 that was conducted within the Newton Division of the LAPD. They measure the levels of criminality within the Newton Division from January 1, 2006 to June 30, 2012 and found a negative correlation between the introduction of LASER and the

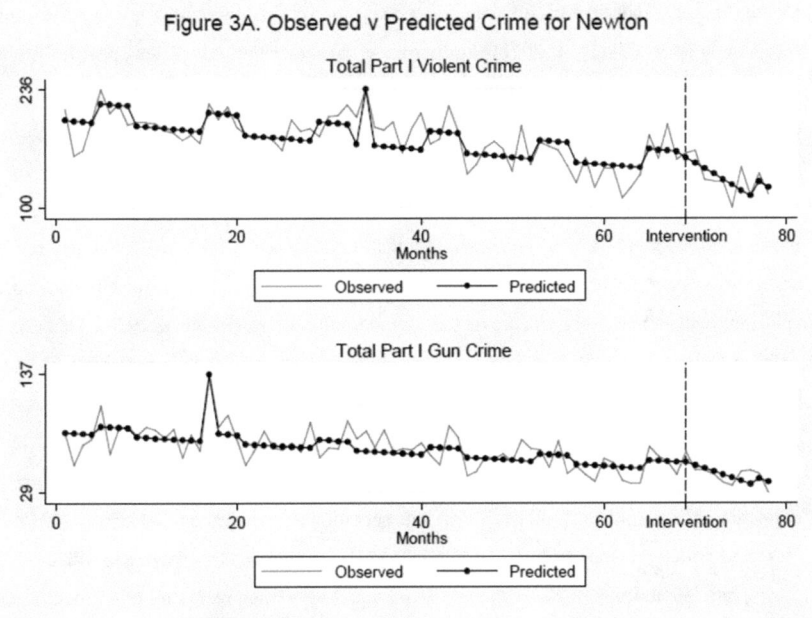

Figure 3: Crime levels of Newton with interrupted time series; Source: Uchida and Swatt 2015, https://journals.sagepub.com/doi/10.1177/1098611113497044

levels of criminality. The drop in gun crime accounted for a decrease of 5.2 % per month after the introduction of the LASER program (Craig & Swatt, 2013). Especially, homicide rates decreased dramatically after the LASER introduction.

Expressed in numbers, there was a drop of 22.59% in homicide rates (Craig & Swatt, 2013). The Newton study was also compared to other police districts within LA, that didn´t run the LASER program. The comparison indicated, that the Newton district reduced the crime levels a lot more than other districts without LASER (Craig & Swatt, 2013).

To come to the discriminatory part of the study, it needs to be pointed out what ethnicities live in Newton district. The Newton police district located in the centre of Los Angeles and is densely populated by Hispanics.

Since LASER is based upon previous crime reports, arrests and gang affiliation, it can create a vicious loop for individuals collecting more and more points and rising upwards the chronic offender bulletin (Bhuiyan, 2021). Furthermore, the algorithm calculates specific `problem areas´ that are from specific interest for the local police and might get overpoliced as a consequence (Bhuiyan, 2021). When the specific target area gets now more attention from the police, it can lead to more arrests and new crime data about the individuals than creates a vicious feedback loop with the algorithm. The algorithm can therefore develop a self-enforcing mechanism based on the discriminatory data that it is feed with. But LASER has also revealed some weaknesses in regular field work. Even a normal stop of a person for a regular control can lead to an increase on the score on the offender bulletin list (Bhuiyan, 2021). That can also enforce a label on controlled people without any criminal record to become criminal after being ranked within the offender's bulletin. This concept is called labelling approach in the social sciences. It can lead to a stigma for the overpoliced ethnic group. The consequences of this policing program can be severe for a target area with increased police presence and the collection of random data of people in the specific neighbourhood (Bhuiyan, 2021). The increased police presence in the LASER zone can also lead to deadly encounters with the police during regular controls. In 2016 alone six Black and Latino men were shot in six months in the target areas (Bhuiyan, 2021). According to residents of the targeted neighbourhoods, the high police presence leads to a culture of distrust and develops an `us versus them´ mentality (Bhuiyan, 2021). This can affect the whole community with distrust and can hinder cooperation between the police and the locals.

Furthermore, it need to be mentioned that Palantir was one crucial backbone of the LASER program, since it helped the program to enhance its effectiveness a lot by combining the data from the databases about violent offenders (Bhuiyan, 2021). This is also the reason why there is no need for a specific case study of Palantir in this paper since most other predictive policing methods are based upon the Palantir database, so it is already an inherent element for LASER and PredPol, just to mention the most important examples for the LA district.

4. Conclusion

To conclude this study, the LASER program showed its potential as an effective predictive policing method by reducing crime rates in specific target areas significantly. It also turned out that it has severe long-time effects for the neighbourhoods in the targeted areas. Especially, when it comes to trust between the police and the local citizens. Furthermore, I think that these smart policing programs need to be modified to be more effective and better justified. In addition, it is for the public unclear, if these algorithms consists out of discriminatory elements that can reinforce patterns of inequality. So, the police should reveal at least the basic principle of the algorithm behind Palantir etc. It should be at least clear, what data is weighted most in the rating of an individual when it comes to criminality assessment. Moreover, and what might be at least as important than the first point is, that the data collection process of the police stations must be more efficient and should avoid biased data based on discriminatory elements. If you feed biased data into the computer, it will give you a biased result. A very simple equation. Probably the database is just too broad to give valid results.

These public concerns are becoming more and more present with a further technologically developing world and the expanded introduction of smart policing methods. AI will develop further in future and algorithms will get better with it, but it should be ensured, that the AI is used in a justified way with accountability measurements in place. Especially, public surveillance will advance a lot through face recognition software, drones and surveillance centre. It is also very hard to predict where the boundaries for privacy of data are and how far public surveillance is allowed to reach into our daily lives. That will be a matter of future research. The further AI advances give also more space for the introduction of new discriminatory elements like filter options for public surveillance cameras, to filter for skin colour, gender etc. In addition, with rising surveillance in the public area, a gigantic mass of personal data can be stored in the police databases, i.e., Palantir, without citizens noticing it. On the other hand, it can ensure a quick response to a crime and a high detection rate. However, it should always be secured that the introduction of smart policing tools is equipped with transparency standards and operate based on a standardized pattern. It might be also very helpful to provide the local citizens with more information about the programs to build trust with them to restore trust again. A closer collaboration with the local residents might also mitigate ethnic discrimination issues. This new approach is called DICPF (Data-informed community-focused policing) and needs to be a crucial part of all smart policing programs in future, to avoid racial discrimination and enhance their effectiveness in a sustainable pattern.

Bibliography

Algorithmic Bias: Why and How Do Computers Make Unfair Decisions? (2023). Liberties.Eu. https://www.liberties.eu/en/stories/algorithmic-bias-17052021/43528

Bhuiyan, J. (2021, November 8). LAPD ended predictive policing programs amid public outcry. A new effort shares many of their flaws. *The Guardian*. https://www.theguardian.com/us-news/2021/nov/07/lapd-predictive-policing-surveillance-reform

Craig, U., & Swatt, M. (2013). Operation LASER and the Effectiveness of Hotspot Patrol: A Panel Analysis. *Police Quarterly, 16*, 287–304. https://doi.org/10.1177/1098611113497044

Cushing, T. (2020, Oktober 1). *Palantir Presentations Show How The LAPD Is Able To Turn Tons Of Garbage Data Into Ineffective Policing.* Techdirt. https://www.techdirt.com/2020/10/01/palantir-presentations-show-how-lapd-is-able-to-turn-tons-garbage-data-into-ineffective-policing/

Dr. Beck, A. J. (2021). *Race and Ethnicity of Violent Crime Offenders and Arrestees, 2018.* U.S. Department of Justice.

Kesin, M., & Wadhar, H. (2015). *SYSTEMS AND METHODS FOR KEY PHRASE CHARACTERIZATION OF DOCUMENTS - Patent application* (PALANTIR TECHNOLOGIES, INC. Patent Nr. AG06F1730FI). https://www.patentsencyclopedia.com/app/20150378996

Pallini-Tipton, C. (2023). *Demographics | Los Angeles City Planning*. Los Angeles City Planning. https://planning.lacity.org/resources/demographics

YOUR KNOWLEDGE HAS VALUE

- We will publish your bachelor's and
  master's thesis, essays and papers

- Your own eBook and book -
  sold worldwide in all relevant shops

- Earn money with each sale

Upload your text at www.GRIN.com
and publish for free